Our Senses

HEARING

Kay Woodward

GARETH**STEVENS**
PUBLISHING
A World Almanac Education Group Company

Please visit our web site at: www.garethstevens.com
For a free color catalog describing Gareth Stevens Publishing's
list of high-quality books and multimedia programs, call
1-800-542-2595 (USA) or 1-800-387-3178 (Canada).
Gareth Stevens Publishing's fax: (414) 332-3567.

Library of Congress Cataloging-in-Publication Data

Woodward, Kay.
    Hearing / Kay Woodward.
      p. cm — (Our senses)
    Includes index.
    ISBN 0-8368-4406-8 (lib. bdg.)
    1. Hearing—Juvenile literature. I. Title.
QP462.2.W66   2005
612.8'5—dc22   2004052568

This North American edition first published in 2005 by
Gareth Stevens Publishing
A World Almanac Education Group Company
330 West Olive Street, Suite 100
Milwaukee, Wisconsin 53212 USA

This U.S. edition copyright © 2005 by Gareth Stevens, Inc.
Original edition copyright © 2005 by Hodder Wayland.
First published in 2005 by Hodder Wayland, an imprint of
Hodder Children's Books, a division of Hodder Headline
Limited, 338 Euston Road, London NW1 3BH, U.K.

Commissioning Editor: Victoria Brooker
Book Editor: Katie Sergeant
Consultant: Carol Ballard
Picture Research: Katie Sergeant
Book Designer: Jane Hawkins
Cover: Hodder Children's Books

Gareth Stevens Editor: Barbara Kiely Miller
Gareth Stevens Designer: Kami Koenig

Printed in China

1 2 3 4 5 6 7 8 9 09 08 07 06 05

Picture Credits
Alamy/David Hoffman Photo Library: 4 (David Hoffman),
14 (Harald Theissen); Corbis: title page, 6 (Norbert Schaefer),
imprint page, 18 (Royalty-Free), 9 (Eye Ubiquitous/Robert
and Linda Mostyn), 10 (Jay Dickman), 11, 15 (Richard Hutchings),
16 (Nathan Benn), 17 (Richard T. Nowitz), 19 (Joe McDonald),
21 (Ecoscene/Robin Williams); Getty Images: 5 (Taxi/Alan Powdrill),
8 Taxi/Mel Yates), 22 (left) (Photodisc Blue/Royalty-free),
23 (Stone/Peter Cade); OSF: 20 (M. Wendler/Okapia);
Wayland Picture Library: 22 (right); zefa: cover (Graham French),
12 (Virgo), 13 (A.B./S. Borges). Artwork on page 7 is by Peter Bull.

About the Author

Kay Woodward is an experienced children's author who
has written over twenty nonfiction and fiction titles.

About the Consultant

Carol Ballard is an elementary school science
coordinator. She is the author of many books for
children and is a consultant for several publishers.

CONTENTS

Words in **bold** type can be found in the glossary.

SOUNDS ALL AROUND!

The world is filled with all kinds of different sounds. There are loud noises and quiet whispers. There are high screeches and low rumbles.

A busy playground is a noisy place.

Sounds go into the ears.

Our **sense** of **hearing** allows us to **listen** to the many amazing sounds around us. We use our ears to hear.

HOW YOUR EARS WORK

Sound travels through the air and into your ears.
Information about the sound is sent from your ears
to your brain. The information helps your brain know
what the sound is. This is how you hear things.

Cover your ears with your hands.
What can you hear?

This is what an ear looks like from the inside.

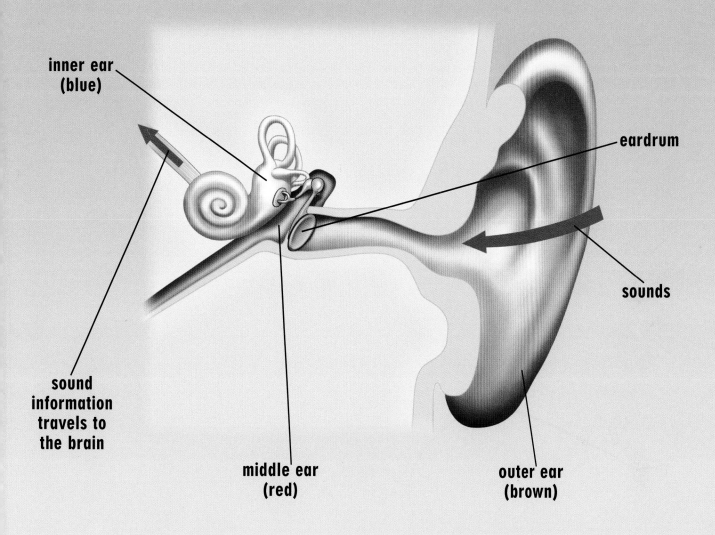

inner ear
(blue)

eardrum

sounds

sound
information
travels to
the brain

middle ear
(red)

outer ear
(brown)

An ear is made up of three parts. The **outer ear** is the part you can see. It is separated from the **middle ear** by the eardrum. The middle ear and the **inner ear** are inside your head. All parts of the ear are connected.

LOUD AND QUIET

Sounds are made when something moves. Small movements make quiet, or soft, sounds. If you hit drums lightly, you will make a soft sound. But if you bang the drums, you will make a loud noise.

Very loud sounds can harm ears. People who have noisy jobs must protect their ears. They wear **earmuffs** to stop too much sound from getting into and harming their ears.

HIGH AND LOW

Some sounds are high, and others are low.
When people scream, they make high sounds.
When people snore, they make low sounds.

Singers use their voices to make lots of sounds. The sounds they sing can be very high or very low. How many different sounds can you sing?

MUSICAL SOUNDS

Musical instruments can make many sounds. Different instruments are played in different ways. You blow air into a recorder. You can change the sounds the recorder makes by covering its holes with your fingers.

You play a guitar by plucking or strumming its strings. When you press the keys on a piano, hammers inside the piano hit strings to make different sounds.

HEARING CLEARLY

Some people cannot hear very well. Everything sounds muffled and quiet to them. People who cannot hear well may have had an illness or injury that damaged their ears. As people get older, they often lose some of their hearing.

Hearing aids make sounds louder. They fit inside or over the ear and help people hear the world around them more clearly.

Hearing aids can be very small. They may be difficult for people to see.

DEAFNESS

People who are deaf cannot hear. Some people are deaf when they are born. Other people become deaf because of an injury or illness. Some people lose their hearing in only one ear.

Instead of using their voices, many deaf people use their hands to talk. They form signs and signals that stand for letters and words. These hand movements are called sign language. Some people who are deaf can tell what others are saying by watching their lips move.

ANIMALS AND HEARING

Many animals have very good hearing. Unlike people, they can move their ears around to hear even more sounds.

Rabbits can hear very quiet sounds with their large ears.

A bat uses its hearing to tell if an insect is in its path.

Bats send out high sounds, then listen to the **echoes** that bounce back. The echoes help bats know where objects are around them.

INSECTS AND HEARING

Some insects do not have ears on the sides of their heads. Instead, these insects hear sounds through other parts of their bodies.

The short-horned grasshopper hears sounds through the sides of its body.

Many insects hear with their legs. Crickets have ears on their front legs. Spiders, who are related to insects, use hairs on their legs to feel sound movements.

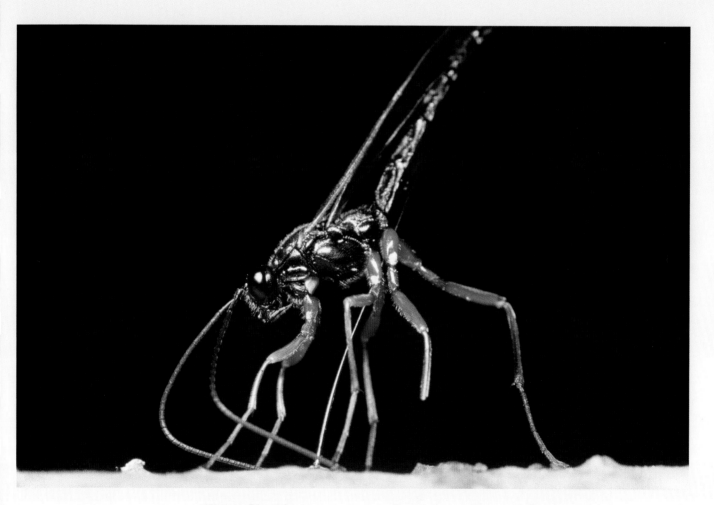

This fly hears sounds through its feet.

CAN YOU GUESS THE SOUND?

Our five senses — hearing, sight, smell, taste, and touch — tell us about the world around us. What happens when we lose one of our senses?

1. Cover your eyes. Now try to recognize different sounds using only your sense of hearing. Can you tell the difference between musical instruments by how they sound? Can you recognize different people's voices?

2. A version of the game "Blind Man's Bluff" was first played about one thousand years ago. To play this game, tie a blindfold around your eyes and ask your friends to stand in different places around the room. When someone calls your name, point to where the voice is coming from. Now take off your blindfold. Were you right?

GLOSSARY

earmuffs: thick pads worn over the ears, which help stop loud sounds from harming a person's hearing

echoes: sounds made when an earlier sound bounces off something solid and is repeated

hearing: the ability, or sense, to receive and identify sounds

hearing aids: small electronic devices that are put into or over people's ears to help them hear better. Hearing aids make sounds louder and clearer.

inner ear: the part of the ear that sends information to the brain. The inner ear is the part of the ear furthest inside the head.

listen: to pay attention to sounds

middle ear: the part of the ear that is inside the head, behind the thin eardrum

outer ear: the part of the ear on the outside of the head, which collects sound

sense: a natural ability to receive and process information using one or more of the body's sense organs, such as the ears, eyes, nose, tongue, or skin. The five senses are hearing, sight, smell, taste, and touch.

INDEX